Bart ten Berge

The Gift

"Joy is the inner awareness of giving without expecting."

Bob Moore

VeReCreations
Publishing House

To all of the children who were
patient and supportive while I was writing
and of whom I am so proud:
Deirdre, Sven, Rooske, Yedidya, Antonia,
Elisha, Yonadav, Amiad, Yo'ad and
my sweet little Dorriya.
With special gratitude to the love of my life,
Georgina Yael Johnson,
for inspiring, motivating and editing.
Thanks to all who invested time and love
to make this book possible.

The Gift

The 1st of 7 Steps
to a happy and fulfilled life.

BART TEN BERGE

"I dedicate my life to exploring,
refining and expressing my qualities
in as many ways as I can"

The Gift is the 1st in a series of seven books, in which each offers one of the 7 Steps to a happy and fulfilled life.

Cover design by Guy Nawy: guy@castronawy.com

7 Steps to a happy and fulfilled life.

The Dedications.

1. THE GIFT

"I dedicate my life to uncovering, exploring, refining and expressing my qualities unconditionally, in as many ways as I can."

2. THE ROCK

"I dedicate myself to becoming a free individual by taking responsibility for my emotions, feelings, thoughts and actions."

3. THE TRUTH

"I dedicate myself to the awakening of my senses and to be being loyal to the depth of my experience, while also respecting the experience of others."

4. THE WAY

"I dedicate myself to uncovering my voice of conscience and to letting it direct my choices through life."

5. THE LIGHT

"I dedicate myself to opening a connection with my inner light or essence, allowing an increasing sense of unity."

6. THE ONE

"I dedicate myself to acceptance of the male and the female within myself, so that I may make peace between them as I evolve towards wholeness."

7. HUMAN

"I dedicate myself to embracing the manifest without reservation, accepting what is there, both in suffering or bliss, in order to find the middle way in which all can coexist."

Contents

The Gift ~ Introducing... YOU!

"Know that each person is unique in the world... and he would do well to bring his uniqueness to perfection."

Rabbi Nachman of Breslov

Welcome to the first of the Seven Steps - The Gift - in which we open the door marked "Quality".

Each of the Seven Steps is a sphere of inner growth; and each area opens and empowers a process of self-discovery. In following the Seven Steps, it is important to remember that each step is intimately connected to the other six. Each movement into an aspect of inner growth affects the whole - the one palace of our existence has many entrances.

We have made The Gift the first of the Seven Steps, as this is a wide gateway to a conscious process of inner growth. Who would not want to find the gifts they were born with? Who would choose a life in which they are not expressed? How could we find purpose in self-development, if the core qualities we were born with are never to be manifested and expressed outwardly?

The Gift offers ways to discover, integrate and express our unique qualities in daily life. The use of our inborn talents is a fundamental need of living. The failure to express our gifts can lead to depression, a sense of despair, a feeling of waste, low self-esteem and decreased vitality.

Yet, when we are expressing our qualities in daily life, a whole process of learning unfolds: involving the refinement of talents; the development of new qualities; and the lesson of how to use our gifts unconditionally and without abuse. It is a process that moves directly from our innate strengths and one that is suffused with joy.

The expression of our individual qualities brings fulfilment and a sense of purpose to our existence. The process of rediscovering and using our qualities in deeper and more refined ways, is the process of a life-time.

Yet, each moment-by-moment choice we make to "check in" on the inner door marked "quality", is immediately rewarded.

We hope you enjoy The Gift. It describes the giant step we take over a lifetime, and also gives the template for the many tiny steps we take daily in the choices we make.

When we begin to express our gifts and qualities, it changes the atmosphere; indeed it impacts the whole world. The joy around expressing a quality is contagious.

We deeply hope that The Gift will inspire you with a passion to increase your daily choices to express your unique qualities to the world.

"The aim (of education) must be the training of independently acting and thinking individuals who, however, can see in the service to the community their highest life achievement."

Albert Einstein

Free Gifts

"We are each gifted in a unique and important way. It is our privilege and our adventure to discover our own special light."

Mary Dunbar

Every living being is born with a unique pallet of qualities. Plants, animals, birds, fish and insects all bring their own qualities with which they serve the world. The planet itself expresses its qualities in a way that makes it possible to sustain a multitude of life forms.

A plant can have many qualities - its role in nature, its physical form, its healing powers and sometimes its nourishing features - but when it starts to bloom, it puts all its effort in the manifestation of flowers, revealing itself in full beauty. That is when a plant comes to its fullest expression.

Conscious, talking, thinking, creative human beings are also governed by a natural drive to manifest beauty. A flower might sing through the subtle vibrations, yet humans can orchestrate a whole opera. The power behind the need to manifest runs through the stems of us all, whether we accept it or not.

When we humans express our qualities, it makes us flower as well. We become attractive, open, inspired and inspiring, fulfilled, radiant beings. Our experience of living shifts to a deeper, more essential place.

We each have a personal group of qualities which are as unique as our fingerprints. These are the gifts we were born with. A tremendous part of our development involves allowing the unconditional expression of these talents.

Expressing and sharing our qualities brings us to our centre, where there is a strong sense of belonging and connection. When we express our qualities, it is as if we remember who we are. We start to live - alive in the here-and-now - connected with both the depth of ourselves and with what we are expressing into the world.

We all use our qualities daily, to varying degrees. But there are no words to describe the power, joy and magnificence of each individual quality when it is directly and unconditionally expressed. The flesh responds with goose bumps: and we don't each have one gift - we have many! These qualities are free; they are abundant; and they are our part of the shared human responsibility to bring heaven to earth.

The process of uncovering and expressing our unique gifts is a lifetime process. It is also an experience which is available to you right now.

Teacher

The classroom of a schoolteacher with an innate talent to teach has a special atmosphere. Students enjoy the lessons more, and have better results. The class is alive, the students feel connected to the teacher and what he teaches. It is a relief to be in such a lesson; there is an atmosphere of togetherness. Learning makes sense.

Quality Street

> "But it is a cold, lifeless business when you go to the shops to buy something, which does not represent your life and talent, but a goldsmith's."

Ralph Waldo Emerson

Our immature individuality and the loss of connection with the depth of ourselves, sometimes make it hard to remember who we are at core - or to find our special talents.

In the Western world, we have a tendency to look for fulfilment outside of ourselves. We seek happiness in material things, or in status, and expect the world to fill up our empty experience of living. If we are never quite happy, it is the fault of something outside of ourselves: the awful "Because of..." or "if only..."

We tend to search outside ourselves for examples of success, happiness and security. Driven by the need to be part of society - or to belong - we try to mimic what we see as successful.

This is based on a deep insecurity and a fear of never quite truly belonging. Our life becomes increasingly driven by a need to be "OK", admired and accepted. Rejection is to be avoided! If you can't make it, fake it. (Perhaps we could risk just "being" it?)

The opinion of others can constitute a large part of how we value ourselves. How things really are to us, from a place of direct experience, can begin to take second place to how things are perceived from the outside - or how we are judged by "the world". As such, appearance and pretence begins to control our lives more than the content of living!

Yet, just as we need the feeling of belonging, we also have a deep need to feel we are special, and to uphold our individuality.

In this whole dance of survival, we often lose contact with the resources we have inside ourselves. We search outside for relief from our feelings of insecurity and emptiness, but that same "outside" often reflects back our own insecurities.

We see how others see us through the coloured glass of ideas we have about ourselves. In this, we become more and more fixated in a wounded "reality", moving further and further from our own centre.

Entangled in the norms of society and family, we gradually lose our ability to distinguish between what is essential to us and what is not. Our thoughts begin to scramble to adjust to what we believe to be acceptable. In this disorder, we begin rejecting parts of ourselves. These "unacceptable" parts are no longer allowed to exist.

These splits and ruptures within our experience bring us into a constant state of survival. We increasingly rely on our mind to dictate our world: which feelings are allowed and which are not; what we should like and what we shouldn't; what we should think and what we shouldn't. And we still break all our own rules.

This entanglement of projections of the judgements and opinions from the outer world can reach a kind of absurdity. At some stage, the bubble bursts. The great society, the judge, we realize, doesn't really exist. We are the author of it all, and the responsibility is ours. Something of deep value from the depth of us screams: "ENOUGH!"

...and we take a deep breath and begin to live.

Chains of Fear

Miriam is a young therapist. She is finishing her studies which she enjoys a lot. Now it is time to start work. This brings forward a lot of anguish and uncertainty in her: "Who am I to "treat" people? Who will take me seriously?"

Her first client is an elderly lady with anxiety disorder. Miriam has hardly slept the past night, and feels a migraine coming on. She thinks about cancelling the appointment, but her supervisor insists she sees it through.

At the start, Miriam is so nervous that it takes effort to control her voice from trembling. But after a while, she gets caught up in the conversation. She forgets her nervousness, and her headache is gone. She feels deeply engaged and expresses herself with an inner calmness and precision. From somewhere inside, she seems to know exactly how to respond.

Quality and Mind-control

"The intuitive mind is a sacred gift and the rational mind is a faithful servant. We have created a society that honours the servant and has forgotten the gift."

Albert Einstein

Much of what we believe to be the authority of "society" is a projection of the beliefs, ideas and judgements of our own minds. The mind is a superb instrument when it is of service to us. Yet in the location and expression of our qualities it can be our slave-master.

Driven by social fears, the mind becomes rigid and judgemental. The experience of living becomes like a rehearsal, for a second-hand fancy dress. In this abuse of our beautiful mind, the freedom and genius of our thoughts get lost.

Our mind can start to rule our senses to an extent that they become scattered and deformed in their function. We lose contact with the sheer experience of life, and the subtlety of feeling, replacing this by mental force with a constructed, "appropriate" reality of the mind. What actually could be giving us pleasure is announced by the mind as a source of "grief", and so we "adjust" our experience to fit the bill.

To be able to unravel this unhappy mess, we need to reconnect with our authentic inner truth again - to move inside. It is logical that in the first place, we become more authentic when we allow what is actually happening inside us to exist, rather than repressing it with what "should" be happening inside us.

In this, we need to begin trusting our own strength and our ability to deal with life, and (dare we say it) our ability to deal with ourselves. This is found by moving to a position within from which we are able to experience life directly and in the moment.

From here, we have the space to honour the feelings that are really there in us - to honour ourselves.

From this place, the mind is open and resourceful. It doesn't dictate the experience; but follows the experience with a relaxed curiosity in order to learn, understand and enrich the whole.

In order to move inside and to reconnect to our innate gifts, we need to take the mind off its kingly horse by finding our own deeper authority.

The mind so often dictates our direction based on an urge to survive, reacting directly on our fears. Expressing gifts involves moving beyond fear - which divides us from the world - into taking a chance on a depth of truthfulness that allows a deeper level of connection.

We can allow the mind its thoughts, judgements and opinions, but we need to invest in them less. We can hear our internal dialogues, speeches, condemnations or self-justifications, but can relate to them as a chattering old neighbour - not as a final supreme authority. With the demotion of the mind, we also open the possibility for conflicting truths or feelings to coexist.

On this journey, it is important to let experience itself sit behind the wheel, and let the mind be the passenger. Perhaps it will be annoying. Perhaps it will pester you by reading the map or finding shortcuts. But in no time, your beautiful mind will be telling you why your happiness has proven it was always right...

"Only those who will risk going too far can possibly find out how far one can go."

TS Eliot

Qualities Make Sense

"A really great talent finds its happiness in execution."

Johann Wolfgang von Goethe

As we begin expressing our gifts, we have a feeling of rejuvenation. At that moment, we are uplifted, experiencing less fear and heaviness. There is a sense of purpose in life.

Deeply involved in what we are doing, we move away from feelings of inner emptiness and toward a state of fulfilment. Engagement with our qualities opens us up and relocates us to the deeper layers of who we are. These layers are suffused with inner confidence and strength.

When we express our qualities, social fears begin to fall away. We worry much less about the opinion of others. We often feel free, liberated and engaged with something timeless, and hours can pass unnoticed. We stop grasping beyond ourselves towards the "thing" that will bring meaning to our lives as we ourselves become the purpose.

In this, there is a feeling of expansion and immediate fulfilment. Even if we die tomorrow, we will be happy, because we have opened something that feels eternal.

The use of our talents, brings us into the moment. Indeed, when we are acting from our qualities, hours can pass and it can seem like minutes...

Knitting it Perfect

Sara has a quality for knitting: she loves to knit. In her free time she knits for the whole town. At her work as a secretary people know her as a shy, withdrawn person; often insecure and sometimes a bit heavy. They don't know of her secret passion and how she transforms into an enthusiastic, alive person, when she starts to express her gift.

Sara looks forward to every second she can spend knitting. She reads about it, talks about it with her friends, and it is the basis of her social life. Knitting gives her pleasure and a feeling of fulfilment. Sometimes, she regrets when a project is finished even though the end-product is perfect: the whole process of knitting itself seems more important to her than the outcome. Knitting itself and sharing her products with her environment is giving her purpose in life.

Qualities and the heart

"Talent is always conscious of its own
abundance, and does not object to sharing."

Alexander Solzhenitsyn

When we express our qualities, our heart is involved with
each move, creating a feeling of joy and fulfilment. The
heart opens like a gate to a realm of beauty and
unconditional acceptance. The expression of qualities is
not only a source of joy to ourselves, but is moving,
inspiring and joyful for others. It is as if the clouds part
and a clearer light illuminates all.

The products left by the expression of our qualities are a source of inspiration, beauty, wonder and joy, to us and others. We like to surround ourselves with design, music, architecture, art. We enjoy listening to music, going to the theatre, the museum, or seeing a movie. As well as being inspiring, it relaxes us, releases stress, and opens us up externally and to a deeper sense of who we are.

The products of our qualities are all around us, making our life more interesting and adding to our well-being, creating a sense of naturalness, easiness and natural belonging.

The expression of our gifts - and sharing this expression with others - opens the heart, bringing us to a sense of unity with a shared human experience. It makes us happy. It brings a sense of fulfilment. It brings an abundance of energy and a kind of timelessness. It is the "something else" that really matters. Heaven and earth rejoice.

"Be who you are and say what you feel because those who mind don't matter and those who matter don't mind."

Dr. Seuss

How do I find my qualities?

> "Knowing others is wisdom, knowing yourself is enlightenment."
>
> **Lao Tzu**

It is already clear, that in order to uncover our qualities, we need to look inside ourselves. In shifting attention from the outside to the world of inner experience, we begin to attune to an authentic layer of direct experience - to what we really enjoy; and to what brings us pleasure.

Our gifts are alive at the depth of our being, linked to aspects of experience that feel most essential. They arise from an area that can't be possessed or controlled, and that has little to do with pretence or ego. They arise directly from the creative fire of pure experience.

This is a journey based not on ideas but on what truly excites us and what brings us to an open connection with life in the moment.

Following, are some clues that will assist in the treasure-hunt for qualities. After many years carrying beliefs about who we are, the treasures we find can be surprising.

Early dreams and likes

As children, we had a direct connection to ourselves. We were authentic, living purely from our experience of what we liked and needed.

Our actions were spontaneous and less ruled by fears. Young children are spontaneously attracted to subjects connected to their qualities.

If we look back to our younger years and reconnect with the things we really enjoyed doing - with our childhood interests, early dreams and early ambitions - this will give us an indication of where our innate talents are.

Passion

We can locate our qualities in those activities or people, we feel a passion for. Sometimes in conversation, a subject comes forward that makes the person start to glow - he becomes alive and passionate. This matters to him.

There is a deeper involvement, a live curiosity, and an opening up: the communication takes on a greater urgency and a different rhythm. This is when we start to touch a subject which is connected with our qualities.

Qualities often come with passion, enthusiasm and a willingness to engage. What could have been a boring speech suddenly becomes extremely interesting when our qualities are touched.

Attraction

The areas in our environment we are attracted to - where we feel like a fish in water - often reflect inner qualities. Whether it is a high-tech innovation, or a meeting with a street-bum, we find these themes stay with us, so that we tell the story to friends, muse on it before we sleep, or continue to gather related information. We often become self-appointed authorities on the subject.

For many people, for example, a hospital is a place of suffering, anxiety and hope for healing. For some, entering a hospital evokes an inner hunger: the atmosphere feels like home. They look around with more than common curiosity, and possibly feel regret that they are not part of the medical system. Surely, there are some medical qualities there.

We can also be deeply attracted to people who are manifesting the qualities that we need to manifest.

Easiness

Often, we can recognize our qualities in the activities that come easy to us. It can be hard to understand why such tasks are so tough for others! When we are in the joy of our qualities, it feels like the whole world should share it!

Expressing our talents is sometimes so natural to us that we don't realize that these tasks reflect a special quality of ourselves.

When you see different people doing the same job, there can be quite a difference in the amount of effort it takes for each of them. Some are "naturals" and are energized by the work: they are the ones with the best fitting qualities for the job.

"A great deal of talent is lost to the world for the want of a little courage."

Sydney Smith

Quality exploration - some questions

1. Who in your environment do you most admire? What is it about them that you value?

2. What did you deeply want to do when you grew up? (Not what you were told you should do!)

3. What subjects or issues get you excited, or create a lot of anger?

4. What activities come easy to you?

5. When watching TV, what moves you at the depth, or stays with you long after the TV is turned off?

Quality Avoidance

> **"Use what talents you possess; The woods would be very silent if no birds sang there except those that sang best."**

> **Attributed to both William Blake and Henry Van Dyke**

It sounds so easy: do the things we love; invest in activities which are fulfilling; and become a gift to ourselves and our environment. Yet we are able to find a thousand reasons why not to.

Most of these reasons are based on convictions and beliefs we built up according to early experience of acceptance or rejection from others.

"I don't believe in this."

What we believe in becomes our reality, our truth. From all the information that comes to us, we tend to choose those bits that fit into the stories we have made for ourselves about who we are. Our beliefs give structure to our reality, and in that way shape the direction of our lives.

Our mind (that has hopefully already been moved to the passenger seat) is very much influenced by our beliefs. Although many beliefs are shared, each individual perspective of reality is unique.

Our beliefs form our perception of "reality", but beneath the surface, they are never actually fixed: we are constantly evolving and developing. Our beliefs might seem strong and solid as stone, but beneath the level of mind, we are constantly revising them based on experience.

Part of this development takes place through communication with others. It can be very refreshing if someone has a totally different view on a situation - especially when the situation is bringing you down. After a life time of believing "I am no good at painting", it can be awakening to hear another affirm directly: "You are really good at this." We might argue back with our old belief, but something deeper starts to soften.

It is important to respect the beliefs of others. Although we can only move from our own truth, this does not mean our truth is absolute.

Sometimes, we hold onto beliefs which obstruct our development and which are self destructive. Those can be based on decisions we took as a result of trauma or through witnessing the pain of others. The journey within can help uncover our deeper needs and understanding in order to allow such convictions to evolve in a way that they will be of service to us.

"First, I have to put food on the table."

Of course, there are the practical reasons for repressing qualities. Will we financially survive? Are we able to support ourselves and our family?

If we find ourselves in a place that feels like a dead end street - with little joy or fulfilment - often financial fears are holding us hostage to a structure. Our life increasingly feels like an obligation. We lose our creativity and our mind gets increasingly black and white; it's all or nothing.

Financial security is quite important and can't be ignored. But with honesty and creativity, it is often possible to bend our career to a more fulfilling direction.

Sometimes, we have to be patient and build new opportunities with small steps, but investing in this already increases hope, fulfilment and joy. If the work we do is a sacrifice for financial security, at least let it be a conscious one!

Sometimes our fear of disappointment, or concern that we will never be able to reach a place of really expressing our gifts, actively blocks us from taking the first steps.

We might have discarded such inner needs as the stuff of fairy tales - the little miracles that happen to others, but not to us. Could we forgive ourselves if we never tried?

It could be that we planned our career based on financial reasons, building on a belief that our real passion will never give us enough income to survive.

This decision could have been so painful that we smothered our qualities totally, even beginning to resent their expression in others.

"I'm not good enough - I would never get anywhere doing what I love."

Our fear of rejection can sometimes bring us to a position where we actively reduce ourselves, letting go of our personal needs. Instead, we try to fulfil what we believe are the expectations of others - of family or society - in order to avoid being rejected. The opinion of others becomes more important than our own. In our need to belong, to be appreciated, or to be seen, we reach out so strongly that we lose connection with ourselves and our own needs, sometimes to a degree that we have no idea what we are good at, what we are good for, or what the purpose is of living at all...

In a subtle way, we put a benchmark of "success" and "failure" on our right to express our own gifts and our right to be happy. How could we be so cruel to ourselves?

"Who is waiting for my qualities? Everything has been done before."

Everything and everyone is waiting for you (yes, you!) to express your qualities.

When we express our qualities, it opens the heart and we get a feeling connection with what we are doing and with the world around us.

Isolation and loneliness decreases, and we become part of the whole, engaging more and more deeply. We start to care. There is a sharing of love for the miracle of living.

The expression of qualities awakens the unconditional part of us. It helps us move beyond fears and judgements. It brings us to a position where we become a source of light for our environment - in which we can be fully alive.

Although almost everything has been done already, nobody did it your way. There could be a million voices, but your voice is unique. In expressing our qualities, we always add to the world. We not only enrich ourselves, but also everyone around us.

"Isn't it selfish to go for your own happiness"

Is it selfish to create an oasis in the desert? Happiness is a state of being, an overflowing cup, freely shared with our surroundings. It is deeply connected with an openness of heart. It is a blessing to be around a happy person.

Sometimes, we fear losing our happiness – or fear that something will happen to make us unhappy. This fear itself can block us from moving into a more happy way of living.

Such fears can be based on beliefs we took from our environment, sometimes such a belief waxes strong in a family or could be based on a prior disappointment or painful rejection.

There can also be an assumption that when others are suffering, it is selfish to go after our own happiness. First we should make others happy, before investing in ourselves.

In this way, we make our well-being dependent on the well-being of another. We are not allowed to show happiness as long as the other is unhappy. This seems very altruistic but the underlying reasons are often quite selfish; the fear of rejection or confrontation.

To put the condition of our happiness or our right to exist in the hands of someone else actually places the responsibility of our happiness with the other, and in this way we become co-dependent and collectively stuck.

It is the responsibility of each of us to act as an example - an example that will show others it is OK to be authentic, alive, vital and happy!

That is the real altruism: to dare to be happy to add to the happiness of the whole.

Of course, when we can add to the happiness of those we care for, this enlarges our own happiness.

This works best when our heart is an overflowing cup, in the joy of manifesting our qualities, when we share our happiness unconditionally.

"There is so much pain and suffering in the world it is wrong to be happy."

When you are in pain, there can be a great comfort in meeting a happy person: it shows that there are other possibilities in life. A happy person is better able to be compassionate or emphatic: he is not waiting for others to change the world before he opens up.

"Life is not about having fun. It's a very serious matter."

When we regress back to childhood, we find that the things we really loved to do - or that came easy to us - were perhaps not rewarded that much, or were taken for granted: "We know that mathematics comes easy to you but what you should really focus on is your languages."

Maybe we find ourselves in a position that was engineered by our parents to fulfil those dreams that they had to sacrifice. We are not always able to express our qualities in such a position.

This can lead to lack of self esteem and sometimes a loss of connection with our qualities. Our innate strengths can seem unimportant or useless, as if nobody is waiting for them.

In educating children, there is often more emphasis on the things which are difficult or hard, and we develop a belief that this is the real "work" - the rest is just "playing". The reward seems greater and the work more "serious" when we engage in activities which are "difficult." This counts as hard work.

We suffer through this process, focused on the result. If the result is good, everything is good. We delay enjoyment of the moment and postpone life, until some point in the future when we can cash in on the successes. In our daily experience, we thus lose the feeling connection with what we are doing. Only success counts and as we don't really appreciate what we do, the measurement of success is based on the amount of appreciation coming from others.

"I am not good at anything anyway."

This can either be an escape from the responsibility of manifestation, or the voice of low self esteem resulting from a lack of affirmation from authorities in childhood.

We could have begun to really believe that our qualities are worthless: that nothing about us is attractive or needed. This can bring us to a situation of insecurity about ourselves, our role in life, and our purpose in the world. We could also become quite nasty towards others that express their gifts.

If we lose all appreciation of ourselves and life seems one big obligation, appreciation itself can become the prize that is used to control others. At least by rationing and controlling our appreciation, we can have an influence on the world.

> **"Do not squander time, for that is the stuff life is made of."**
>
> **Benjamin Franklin**

Healing Gifts.

> **"To find out what one is fitted to do, and to secure an opportunity to do it, is the key to happiness."**

> **John Dewey**

The use of our talents has quite an influence on our whole system. It increases our vitality and balances us energetically, emotionally, mentally, and also physically.

The expression of our qualities reduces inner conflicts and creates an inner atmosphere of calmness and peace. Authentic expression carries less stress, as it frees us from a constant struggle to be seen, and to avoid rejection. The fear of rejection no longer corrupts our direction.

The more we are able to express our qualities on a daily basis, the more we start to live in the moment, moving out of the stress of survival.

Above all, we become more fulfilled and happy and nothing is as good for our general health as happiness.

Quality Sentience

Miriam, the young therapist, has suffered for years from oversensitive skin. She could not wear certain materials, as her skin would react to them with a rash and great itching. By looking at her, you can tell in her refined appearance that she is a sensitive person. This matches her statement that she has a strong sensitivity for the emotions and feelings of others, which make her feel quite vulnerable. Because of this, she kept some distance from others, and led quite a solitary life.

After quite a difficult start of working as a therapist, Miriam became quite successful. It was amazing to see the difference in her appearance; she looked more earthly, less transparent. Also, the oversensitivity of her skin went down dramatically, she could wear materials she was not able to wear before. She seemed to be much more emotionally balanced. The active use of Miriam's quality of empathy meant that where the quality had earlier caused her suffering, it now gave her strength and greater health.

Qualities: a User's Guide.

"The finest qualities of our nature, like the bloom on fruits, can be preserved only by the most delicate handling."

Henry David Thoreau

The expression of our qualities seems to be one of the main purposes of our human life. Even our physical body is built in a way that it supports the manifestation of qualities. When we are in the flow of expressing our gifts, it adds to our physical well-being and health and opens higher levels of vitality. The use of our gifts encourages a union between body, mind and soul. It has healing effects on the emotional and mental sides of us and brings the heart alive.

Quality Sensitivity

There is a strong connection between our senses and our talents. A musician has a refined sense of hearing. A painter has an amazing ability to differentiate colour. A masseur has a developed sense of touch.

Each quality has its own relation with one or more of our senses. Sometimes, when we are not able to express a talent, the sense which is related to that special quality can go wild.

When there is over-sensitivity in one or more of our senses, it can be an indication that a connected quality is not being expressed.

In expressing this quality, we create a framework in which the sense can operate as it needs to. This can often lead to a healing of the disorder, as the sense gets balanced and the over-sensitivity disappears.

Gift of Vitality

When we are expressing our qualities we move into a higher level of vitality, and our energy seems to be endless.

Our talents are part of our spiritual make-up. They move with a high level of vibration. Expression of this finer vibration quickens our whole energy-system, which gives us a feeling of elation. This quickening releases a lot of basic vitality, which gives the feeling of endless energy.

A lack of vitality is sometimes associated with depression.

When we are in depression, everything can seem pointless. It is as if we live in a bubble, or a vacuum. The connection with the world around us begins to break down.

The capacity to feel diminishes, to be replaced by a dark, background sensation, and sometimes a feeling of doom. There is a terrible feeling of emptiness. All the energy in the chest area is stagnant.

The first and most important thing to do when we are in depression is to create movement: physical movement, emotional movement and any form of movement.

Then (sometimes with the help of medication), we can start to express some quality, which even in small ways, increases vitality, reopens our connection with the world, and is of immense help to move out of depression and back into life.

Qualities and the Right to Exist

When we are using our talents, we are deeply connected with what we are doing and what we are doing feels totally right.

The expression of our qualities creates a feeling of being the right person, at the right place, at the right time. Fears fall away, as when we are "in" our qualities, there is no question about our right to exist - we just unconditionally exist in the moment. We move towards a harmony within ourselves and a unity with our environment.

As children, we formed ideas about our right to exist in the family, and later in the world, which were based on the appearance of success and the amount of appreciation we receive. The natural, unconditional right to exist - and to authentically express what we are at the depth - became gradually eroded.

This dependency on the appreciation of others can create a deep rage - which is often directed against ourselves, as self destructiveness.

We do not allow ourselves to make mistakes; we tell ourselves we are not good enough; we are mean with self-appreciation like a cruel school mistress. When the world appreciates us, we often feel we stole something, as if we are guilty of hiding the "failure" we secretly are.

By giving others the authority over our rights to express, to feel successful, to really enjoy ourselves, we lose the freedom to play, to investigate, to make mistakes, and to be what we are.

In losing the feeling connection with our role in life, we lose a lot of pleasure in what we are doing and life becomes a burden, very serious indeed.

Some qualities are totally ignored because our parents or the system could see no future employment in them, or because they were simply outside the educational syllabus (for example, the quality of "naughtiness"). They are so far from "serious" that they can be of no service to society (as it is) and therefore are deemed to have no value.

Qualities show you're special

It is important to remember that there are qualities in the whole range of human expression and that each individual has his own unique combination. Although some individuals seem to share the same qualities, the expression is always unique.

Each composer has his own style; no piece of music is the same. It is like a fingerprint - we can recognize the composer through his music just as we can recognize through the taste of the wine the area and the grapes of the vine.

The use of our talents is helpful to build an individuality which is based on our own natural uniqueness. This makes us special, but not more or less special than any other human being.

Only when our individuality matures to a point where we are able to take responsibility for our own emotions, feelings, thoughts and behaviour, do we reach a state in which we are a free individual.

From this point, we are able to appreciate and respect the individuality of others. Then union is possible without getting entangled, free of the need to control or to be controlled. We are one, but we are not the same.

In the background of a lot of personality disorders we often see a deep confusion around the whole issue of individuality and union. Often, we find a person deeply lost in social entanglements in which the whole issue of self-acceptance and rejection is played out in a big way.

The right to be an individual becomes dependent on the social environment, at the same time as it is in a perpetual struggle with "social" norms. At the other extreme, the drive to come to union with another person can become border-less in which individual needs get lost in social entanglement.

To differing degrees, we can all get caught in wounds connected with an early loss of self esteem within the family structure. In this, the natural build up of individuality was damaged, creating wounds that play out in adult life. This can make social connection feel unsafe, and is often expressed in a strong need to control. A person is literally stuck between the need to find union, and the need to be special, and is not really able to move in either direction.

Aside of therapy to heal wounds from early childhood, it is of great benefit in the whole healing process to invest in expressing the talents.

When Maths is Easy.

Mathematics is exactly Jack's piece of cake: a little explanation is enough to get her going. It is beyond her understanding that other students are not getting it. She has very little patience with them; it seems so logical to her, they must be morons.

Advanced Quality Considerations

"Talent is God given. Be humble. Fame is man-given. Be grateful. Conceit is self-given. Be careful."

John Wooden

When we are on the way of expressing our talents, a whole learning process starts: a process that is connected with the integration of the use of our qualities, the refinement of our talents, and the development of new qualities.

Although this journey is unique for everyone, there are some more general issues that could be considered, in order to affirm this process.

Insecurity

In expressing our qualities, we express from the depth of ourselves. We really care about what we are bringing outward, it is part of ourselves, as well as being part of something much greater than us. There is a natural integrity in what we are doing.

At the same time, when we are just beginning to express our qualities, we can feel quite vulnerable. Before - and after - using our talents, we can suffer from deep fears and insecurity - even though in the moment of expression we felt great.

When we use our talents on a regular basis however, the uncertainty and the fears begin to give way to a deeper trust and inner strength - a beautiful strength that can contain a natural vulnerability. This vulnerability is connected with the intimate authenticity of expression and with the accompanying openness and integrity. This vulnerability is not a weakness, but strength: the strength of purity.

Quality Integration

There is a whole learning process connected with the integration and refinement of quality expression in daily life. The more we use our qualities, the more our personality undergoes a positive transformation. But also, the qualities themselves move through a whole cycle of development.

When we express our talents, they gradually begin to integrate into our personality.

The passion, inspiration and fulfilment linked to quality manifestation becomes part of our daily life experience. This brings us to a position where we are more self-secure, open-hearted and have a clearer direction in life.

Having passed the initial hurdles to quality manifestation - such as insecurity, social resistance and fear of disappointment - we find ourselves far more self confident.

Nobody else can give us this self confidence. It develops out of choices to move from our own deeper needs - strengthening our sense that we are able to deal with life.

Our talents attune us to our deepest direction in life. They take us to a place where we feel connected and "at one" with what we do. We become the right person, in the right moment, at the right time.

Our qualities move from an unconditional place inside ourselves and lead us - if expressed freely - back to that place. It is a process that supports the opening of the heart, increasing our wisdom and diminishing the need to be judgemental.

We become more able to receive what is really before us, and less addicted to dictating what we want to be there. We become more unconditional towards ourselves and the world - which means that with increased options and freedom, our world enlarges.

Quality Refinement.

In the expression of our qualities, we move through a whole cycle of development. When we start expressing a new talent, we have to create a structure in which we are able to express that quality. Guided by this quality, we find a place, a time, and a means to integrate that talent into our lives. When we want to start expressing a quality, we need the right form to bring this quality into the world.

For a musician, this will mean selecting the right instrument, finding a teacher, and making time to play. Through expressing this new talent, we learn from the talent itself how it needs to be expressed in its purest form. Through increasing our abilities to use this talent and adjusting to what feels the best way to express ourselves, we can come to a point where we become one with the means to express our gift.

Most of the time, this is hard work. At the same time, we see that the quality itself is getting more and more refined in its expression. This leads to a situation where we are able to surrender to the quality: we are becoming the instrument through which the quality is expressing itself: an open channel for the quality. This is pure bliss.

Something new

In the process of integration and refinement of a quality, we learn to channel a quality authentically, and we can come to a point where we master it.

This is when the talent is integrated into our personality in such a way that it becomes part of our nature. The expression of the quality is quite natural and becomes less exciting.

In the passion to share the experience, we often then meet the need to teach others how to express and develop this talent. This gives us the chance to deepen our understanding as to how this quality works, and how its refinement and development works through others.

It also means we need to develop teaching skills, or perhaps skills in communication. Either we pull in a quality which is already in us, or we begin to develop a whole new quality. In both cases, we often move through the whole cycle of integration and refinement again. With the same hard work, the new talent also becomes part of our nature.

This is just one example of how - when we begin to manifest qualities - our whole range of qualities begins to expand. In the expansion of all we are, we pull in and develop new qualities on the strength of a gift we are already using.

It is difficult to develop a new talent, if we are not expressing any of our qualities at all yet. It is always best to start out with some quality (no matter how small) we know we already have.

Some people are gifted with a great number of talents without a clear leading talent. They can feel attracted in many different directions and it can be confusing for them to choose where to begin.

With so many possibilities available, it is helpful to start to express only one or a few qualities to the depth, and then move with life as it often leads them to the place where they really need to be.

Quality Burn-out.

An important part of human development involves the integration of our qualities into our personality. This goes together with an opening of the heart, in which our gifts begin to flow through us unconditionally.

This naturally takes us to a space where we realize that our gifts are there to be used, without the interference of fears and without the need to identify with our qualities as being our personal possession.

Sometimes, we are wounded in our personality in a way that the natural development towards an unconditional use of our qualities gets complicated. We begin using our qualities in a more selfish, fear based way; sometimes to a point that we abuse our talents to control or manipulate, or to gain a sense of superiority. It could also be that this happens under the influence of an outer authority.

This can create a crisis in which the heart starts to close, and we become anxious or depressed as it becomes more and more difficult to express our gifts.

It can be a kind of quality burn-out. This creates an opportunity to do some work on ourselves, and to start healing our personality to a point that we feel safe enough to open our heart again.

In this, we might need the courage to revisit some traumatic experience of our past that we were not able to integrate at that time. Those experiences can have a big impact on our beliefs and how our mind works. What we construct as reality in our beliefs, is our truth, and the fortress we live in. Our choice is to trust unconditionally in our quality and to use this strength to heal the parts of ourselves that have been trapped.

Quality Traps

> **"Great talents are the most lovely and often the most dangerous fruits on the tree of humanity. They hang upon the most slender twigs that are easily snapped off."**
>
> **C. G. Jung**

Our beliefs influence how we perceive and relate to the world around us. They give direction to our senses and how information is processed by the mind. The more we are in survival mode as a result of trauma or fear; the more we base our truth on beliefs powered by fear.

The mind takes charge, and dictates experience according to those beliefs. In such situations, we can lose touch with the deeper, experience of life which based on the natural ethics of the heart. Basically, we lose touch with ourselves and start living in a bubble in which our truth becomes the truth and our perception of reality becomes the reality.

Sometimes, we are wounded in a way that the mind keeps the heart active: constructing the feelings of the heart and through the heart, abusing qualities for its own survivalist reasons.

There is no unconditional sharing, but love and qualities are used and abused. Our wounded position - and the reflection of that on our beliefs - is the reality we stand for and from which we relate to the world. In this way, seemingly altruistic motives can lead to great destructiveness.

If we abuse our qualities in this way, the joy and fulfilment arising from the expression of our gifts gets lost and is sometimes replaced by the pleasure it can give us to have power over others. When we are caught in patterns like this, we see a growing imbalance on all levels and a process of inner decay, which often leads to self destruction.

Where we try to change the world from our wounds, we only seem to create similar wounds around us.

After experiencing processes like this, there is sometimes a strong fear to express any quality at all. We become afraid to lose ourselves in a similar way and lose trust in ourselves and in our ability to use our talents in a different way - without causing harm.

All this makes it important to take responsibility for our own wounds through working on our healing process. It doesn't matter how famous or successful we are, the spiritual challenge is the same.

Law and Disorder

By studying hard, Jez became a lawyer. The choice for this profession was based on what seemed all-important at the time: to make his mother proud, to make a good living to support a family, to achieve the social status.

Every day, Jez has to go to work. It feels like an obligation and a burden. At work, it is quite a struggle to get the job done right. It seems unfair that his colleague does the job with such an ease and flair - the harder the case the more he seems to enjoy it. He gets much more appreciation and respect, although it looks like Jez puts much more effort into his cases, preparing them for hours and hours. It is hard work and not really fulfilling. He is living for the free weekends and holidays - of which there never seems to be enough. The easy life Jez expected in his choice of profession feels like imprisonment.

Beyond the Limits

"Everyone has talent. What is rare is the courage to follow the talent to the dark place where it leads."

Erica Jong

During the integration of our talents into our personality, we can meet several difficulties. It is important to realize that the expression of our talents leads us gradually to our centre, towards the depth of ourselves. This is an inner journey, which in order to deepen, must also sometimes confront where we are wounded - the walls that lead to the distance in the first place.

For better or worse

One clear obstacle we can meet on this pathway is insecurity.

When we are able to deal with our insecurity and contain it, we come to a place of purity in which we are more open-minded and humane. This occurs as growing self esteem, creates a space from which we can realize that our truth is not the only truth and that everybody is reflecting a part of a much greater truth. We become more open, as we deepen our insight of others as complete and equal human beings.

It is only where we get entangled, as a result of an inner fight with our own insecurity that we risk falling into the trap of superiority or haughtiness used as a cover up of the forbidden inner insecurity.

We get caught in being the best, and if we can't be that, we will be the best at being the worst. This movement has been described as a swing between being the most grandiose human, to being a worm. Often the result can be a "grandiose worm"!

"Everyone" hates me.

In expressing our qualities more unconditionally, we will be confronted with our social fears - and will have to deal with them. Our social fears are awoken by an unwillingness to face the pain of rejection: the pain of not been seen.

If we can accept this pain and contain the rage which comes with it, we will uncover a deeper freedom and an ability to be truthful to ourselves and the world. This opens the way for us to manifest ourselves in a natural, open and honest way - perfectly imperfect.

When we get entangled with these fears and the underlying pain, we can fall into the trap of pretence or deceit. In this, we risk a worse suffering through fruitless, frustrating ego-struggles, control-issues and power games.

MORE applause!

At our base, we can meet wounds around our right to exist. These wounds conspire around the illusion that we have to "deserve" or "earn" our right to exist, and that others have to give it to us. Yet, no global fan-club or universal popularity can heal this wound. It is between the depths of us and existence itself.

There tends to be a great amount of rage and aggression around the right to exist and the lack of self-esteem resulting from such fundamental wounds. If we are able to accept the emotion, contain the pain and aggression, it will support us in becoming a free individual, with the ability to put borders where needed.

When we assume an unquestioned right to exist, we become more able to truly and authentically stand for ourselves. We tap into the power of an unquestioned right to manifest ourselves from the depth.

In addition, we are more able to give others the total freedom to manifest their qualities. This is no longer a competition or a threat to us. It is a shared celebration.

If we get entangled in this wound, there can be a deep dependency on the affirmation of others.

Sometimes, this wound can express itself in patterns of care taking - we take care of others in a way that creates a dependency. Instead of supporting them to stand on their own feet and to come into their strength, we attempt to take over the responsibility for their lives - weakening them rather than strengthening!

Such patterns are based on a deep need for affirmation within ourselves. At a certain point, it can all become too much and we become reproachful or aggressive. We are not seen. No gratitude!

Another stumbling block arising from a wounded right to exist is seen where we move into patterns of competition. The success or failure of the "other" becomes the factor that defines us, more than our own joy in expression. This "you or me" thinking can propagate, creating strata of judgement, aggression and rejection of whatever does not fit into our reality. With the loss of joy, comes a loss of ability to directly manifest our gifts, and a deepening loneliness.

Where's the prize?

The reward of expressing qualities is in the first place always in the joy of expression.

So why do we miss public approval? This craving for affirmation can arise out of wounds around authority and guilt. At some stage - perhaps early on - our view of authority took a blow. We understood authority as someone who has power over us, deciding matters in our lives and telling us what to do and how to do it. From a wounded perspective, authority could be seen as part of a power structure, riddled with obligation, guilt and the power to approve or condemn.

A natural, authentic authority is given freely to those who are a little further on the pathway in a particular aspect, and who have a position in which they can inspire or support us to find our own way.

When we are confused about authority, we lose the freedom to be spontaneous and to choose to move from our own inner authority. We can lose sight of the basic need to move through our own lessons of life according to our own rhythm.

We can create a virtual authority in our mind that dictates us through norms, black and white, obligation and self-degradation. We lose connection with our inner discipline and become increasingly unreliable and unable to commit. We get addicted to an outer authority telling us what is right and wrong; and we become normative.

Because we begin to "pretend" so as to be "OK" in the view of the imagined outer authority, we get trapped in structures of guilt and have an increasing difficulty taking any responsibility at all.

Authority issues often involve confusion around the issue of responsibility. It becomes difficult to differentiate between what we can be responsible for, and what is the responsibility of others.

In our lack of clarity, we might be crying about saving Africa, at the same time that we let down our own friends. The empowering process of healing around the issues of responsibility and freedom are addressed in more depth in the 2nd Step ~ The Rock.

Authority confusion often manifests when we have been in a situation in which we relied on an authority and were disappointed, losing trust in authority altogether. If we are able to accept this wound and contain the pain, we will be lead back to our own inner authority.

Accepting our vocation as the authors of our own attitude to living, we can develop an ability to feel what is truly right for us and what not. We learn to recognize when to accept the support of others, and when to go on alone.

We become more attuned to our own needs, finding discipline when needed and recruiting help from others as required. We learn to take our own decisions and follow them through, taking responsibility for both failure and success in a process of learning and discovery.

Jez's Secret Gift

Let us return to Jez. At work, Jez is stressed at how he is perceived by others. In particular, one gifted colleague makes him insecure. Although he always fantasized about becoming a stand-up comedian, on his mother's "advice" he became a lawyer. She recognized his talent to speak and improvise in public and thought this would make him an excellent advocate.

It is true that Jez enjoys speaking in the courtroom, but even then, he is constantly bothered by the impression he makes on others. Is the judge taking him seriously? Is he representing his client well enough? Is his insecurity visible? He never feels free.

One day, his gifted colleague asks Jez to do something 'funny' at the goodbye party of one of his senior partners. Jez accepted the challenge.

At the night of the party, he took the piss of his office, his talented colleague and especially of himself. For the first time, he felt totally free, and "seen" by his colleagues. He experienced a great elevation and did not worry for a second what his colleagues would think of him.

The Empty Fortress.

As we begin to express our qualities, we could encounter a wound around intimacy, connected with feelings of loneliness, of being socially unsafe and a sense of inner coldness. This can often be connected with sexual problems and reflected outwards in sexual difficulty.

The irony is, that the inner fortress we create to protect ourselves against the pain of intimacy, is often uninhabited - even we do not live there! In moving into that space ourselves, with the sincere intent to express the depths of ourselves, the sense of isolation and fear of intimacy can already be greatly relieved.

In a situation where we feel isolated from the rest of the world, loneliness increases as we long for a basic togetherness. We tend to look for solutions outside ourselves, hoping that a special connection with another will fulfil us and will take away our loneliness. But the real problem lies in our difficulty to let others in - or even to "go there" ourselves.

We can be in a position where we give a lot to others and the world and this is our way to get a sense of connection - especially with those who receive from us. But still, this does not take away our loneliness.

In the place of vulnerability, we seek to control. The difficulty to let others in is often connected with fears of helplessness and a deep self rejection. When another person comes close to our inner sealed fortress, it can provoke fear, repulsion and sometimes a lot of confusion.

We can have an intense fear of being possessed which can cause us to try and take control by finding a way to possess the other.

Where we are not able to experience real union or togetherness, we tend to hold on to things or to other people, to give us a sense of safety. Especially when there has been some experience of togetherness or union, the urge to posses can appear with a vengeance in order to protect ourselves from facing our wounds around intimacy.

Meeting the Lone Wolf

Loneliness is part of our human make-up connected with the loss of the experience of union. When we move to deeply into loneliness we start to move in isolation. It becomes difficulty to build bridges to others or to let others in. We start to isolate ourselves and lose connection with the world around us. It is as if we are on an island, outside of our social environment. In this way loneliness can lead to depression.

It can be very healing to connect from our loneliness to the loneliness of others. We all have loneliness inside us: it is a shared human experience. To become aware of this opens the heart and brings forward feelings of compassion or empathy. Moving us back towards union.

If we are able to accept and to contain our pains and fears around intimacy, we can find a way to start to experience union with the world around us.

We can find a position where we are able to distinguish the union between us behind all the differences. It places us in a situation where we are able to accept, contain and enjoy the differences connected with each background and personality.

In experiencing union, we are able to let go of the urge to possess, and we become aware of the equality between people and all life forms.

When we are entangled in our wounds and fears around intimacy it can bring forward a strong possessiveness, deep entanglement in jealousy and difficulties to let others close.

We need to be "special" to be admired. Individual differences are experienced as a threat. There can be a strong urge to dominate others and the world around.

Often, we suffer from deep feelings of loneliness and isolation, and we can move in patterns of sexual self-abuse.

When we move into expressing our qualities - even using our qualities to express the depth of our pain, a kind of transformation occurs. Even if we are physically isolated, we open a connection with creation itself, and find a place within the great orchestra of the whole.

When we share our qualities with others, the invitation to intimacy is opened, like a door within a fortress at the depth of ourselves. Even if our invitees refuse to walk through, other guests, attracted by the allure of an authentic quality, will come.

Human Suffering

Physical, emotional, mental and spiritual suffering is more or less part of our life experience. It seems that there is a lot of fear and judgement around suffering, that pain should involve shame.

When a person is in pain, we tend to find all kind of reasons why this is happening to this specific person. Often these reasons are moving into judgement, "it is the persons own fault, it is because of..."

Based on our own fears of suffering, we become quite cruel towards each other, as when there is judgement, there is little compassion. Our judgements so often place a suffering person in a position of isolation and shame. "He got this terrible cancer because - (of all the behaviours that mean it won't happen to us...)"

This collective fear of suffering has quite an influence on our personal attitude towards ourselves when we are in pain. It seems that something is wrong with us, we have to get rid of our suffering as soon as possible and if this is not possible, we have to hide it.

When we are in a grief-process or in chronic physical, emotional or mental distress, we don't talk about it after a while, as it becomes difficult to bother people again and again with the same stories. And indeed, in such situations we begin losing social connections.

Our inner fight with our pain, often adds to our suffering. We move into despair and panic in our suffering. We lose self-confidence.

When we are in pain, it often places us in a situation where we stop living. We get deeply entangled in our suffering, feel that something is wrong with us, that we are being punished and sometimes we feel a rage with others, with existence or with god.

We place ourselves in a situation of "either-or". We deny ourselves moments of joy, happiness, fulfilment, spiritual elevation and light, because first, that suffering has to be completely gone.

Happily there is help out there. There are painkillers and other medicines, and a lot of different kinds of physical, emotional, mental and spiritual therapies which can help us to make our life more bearable

It is important to understand that our suffering often gives us the opportunity to move more deeply inside ourselves. It can teach us what is more and what is less essential in our lives. Suffering often has a clarifying effect which brings us back to our centre and helps us let go of a lot of entanglements we can find ourselves in, in daily life. It has the power to purify.

When we are able to accept our suffering as part of our lives and are able to contain it, with or without help of medication or other forms of support, it helps us build self-confidence to be able to deal with life. It brings us more clarity about what is essential and not essential in our lives. It helps us to free ourselves from daily life and inner entanglements.

It opens us up to be more understanding, compassionate and emphatic.

To be able to contain the more painful side of life reduces the fear of suffering and enables us to contain the suffering of others.

If we get entangled in our suffering, our pain becomes the centre of our existence. In our struggle to become free of it, we often move into a far deeper suffering than is necessary.

In the inner fight against our pain, we often isolate ourselves and it becomes more difficult to reach out for help. We lose self-confidence and move in structures of self-rejection. We feel inferior.

There is a tendency to become very self-centred and to move into victim-hood. Sometimes, our suffering is used to give us a special status or to give us some special rights. In this case, it is even more complicated to let go of the entanglement in the suffering. It is possible that we become bitter, angry people with a grudge against life and the whole world. Trauma defines us, and we will fight for that place to stand.

If we get entangled in the fears around suffering, we become intolerant towards the pains of others. We don't want to be confronted with it. We lose our ability to be compassionate or empathetic. We lose self-confidence to deal with life, sometimes masked by a superior attitude. "You're in pain? Welcome to MY world!"

All these lessons in life have the potential to get us out of balance as we get deeply entangled with inner fights, leading to a closure of the heart.

In those cases the free, unconditional expression of our qualities becomes difficult, as we lose joy and fulfilment in expressing them.

Yet at the same time - if we are able to hold on to some free and unconditional expression of our talents - we find we can move more easily through these challenges.

Sometimes we have to find or develop a totally new way to bring our gifts into the world. For example from Edgar Elgar's Pomp and Circumstance before World War 1 - full of optimism and national pride - through to his Cello concerto - swimming with depth, grief and feeling in the aftermath of the war.

The main principle in meeting blocks around quality expression, is to try to accept them; take responsibility for them; and keep track of what is most essential in your life. For sure the expression of your gifts is part of that.

Conclusion

"The best and most beautiful things in the world cannot be seen or even touched. They must be felt with the heart."

Helen Keller

Our qualities are part of our spiritual make-up and each individual has their own set of talents. In expressing our gifts, we serve ourselves, and we serve others. Expression of our talents give us a sense of purpose and direction in life. In expressing our qualities, we become more vital and more alive, moving increasingly unconditionally into the "here and now". Sharing our talents gives us an experience of belonging and of happiness.

To come to the depth of expressing our talents in a pure and unconditional way, is a lifelong quest with many twists and turns. Through this process, parts of us which were asleep will come to life. We will encounter old wounds and hurdles that need to be managed, and we will discover ever wider possibilities and dimensions of ourselves.

There will be many inner and outer adventures and challenges. Our ability to deal with them and learn from them, brings us self-confidence, insight, wisdom, freedom, unity and above all - the natural ability to be ourselves in an open and free way.

The more we are able to express our gifts unconditionally, the more we move to the depth of ourselves - finding fulfilment and union within and with the universe around us. It will bring us to our full potential. Life has a purpose.

The discovery and expression of our talents enables us to recognize the gifts of others. A society that celebrates the qualities of each individual and supports the expression of talent is a happy, healthy society. It is an individual step, and a step humanity needs to take as a whole.

The Rock

The 2nd Step in the 7 Step series.

"I dedicate myself to becoming a free individual by taking responsibility for my own emotions, feelings, thoughts and actions."

The Rock is the foundation of the process of inner growth. On our way to becoming free individuals, we develop self-confidence and an unconditional right to exist; and this moves us beyond our fears of rejection. Through this process, we can become free and natural human-beings - open to learn and develop.

The dance into freedom moves through the rhythm of our choices to take responsibility.

The more we are able to take responsibility for our thoughts, feelings, emotions and actions, the more we take charge of our lives. This brings the freedom to enjoy life fully without reserve; and to learn through living. It brings us the opportunity to become masters of our attitude and to vitalize, widen and enrich our experience of living.

The 2nd Step, The Rock, moves us through a process of transformation, enlarging our ability to respond to life from our abundant strength as free individuals in union with our fellow men and our planet.

"Freedom is not worth having if it does not include the freedom to make mistakes."

Mahatma Gandhi

About Bart ten Berge

7 Steps to a happy and fulfilled life is a teaching method in inner growth developed by the Dutch spiritual teacher and healer Bart ten Berge. The basis of this method is grounded in his medical and psychological studies.

During Bart's study in psychology and classical homeopathy, a health challenge in his own family led him to Robert Moore. Mr. Moore, a renowned energy healer in Denmark, was successful where all others had failed, and Bart became interested in the whole field of energy-healing.

For the next 20 years, Bart studied with Robert Moore and became a prominent energy healer in his own right. He founded Chashymie Centre for Spiritual Healing in Holland where he still maintains a large private practice of international clients. He also developed The Practice of Healing, a seven-year curriculum that introduces students to the art and science of energy healing and inner-growth.

Bart's latest offering to the world of inner growth and self-development brings seven, practical pillars of wisdom that act as openings to the infinite resources of the human soul. Grounded, inspiring and designed for application, 7 Steps is an invitation to all awake souls to open those inner doors that will enrich and deepen the experience of living.

For more information on Bart and the 7 Steps series of books and training, visit www.Inner-Growth.org.

List of Talents:

> **"When you start using your gifts and talents to earn a living, you naturally gravitate towards work you are naturally great at and can excel at."**
>
> **"It's kind of fun to do the impossible."**
>
> **Walt Disney**

The amount of qualities we collectively bring into the world is overwhelming. The number of our shared gifts is not static but dynamic. There is constant movement as new qualities are developed and older talents cease to be expressed. Each individual expression of a quality is unique in itself, with its own specific flavour. Imagine the crime, then, to never offer outwards that which only *you* can express!

Following, is a list of qualities to serve as an inspiration. These are just a sample of the infinite repertoire of human gifts.

There can be a gift: to Act, to Adept, for Adventure, for Ambition, to Analyse, to Arbitrate, to Articulate, for Austerity, to Budget, to Bridge, to Build, to Care, to Channel, for Charisma, for Cinematography, to Classify, to Clean, to Commit, to Compete, to Complete, to Compose, to Conduct, to Communicate, to Cook, to Cooperate, to Coordinate, to Counsel, for Craftsmanship, to Create, to Deal with animals, to Deal with children, to Deal with feelings and emotions, to Deal with plant life, to Decide, to Design, to Diplomacy, to Discriminate, to Discipline, to Disengage, to Edit, for Efficiency, for Electronics, for Empathy, for Engineering, to Entertain, to Escort, to Estimate, to Evaluate, to Expedite, to Fight, to Find, for Friendship, to Generate ideas, for Generosity, to Giving presents, to Go with the flow, for Gratuitousness, to Guard, to Guide, to Handle power, to Harmonize, to Have fun, to Heal, to Help, to Host, to Imagine, to Implement, for Industriousness, to Initiate, to Innovate, to Inspire, to Interview, to Invent, to Investigate, to Judge, to Keep record, for Kindness, for Languages, for Leadership, to Learn, to Legislate, to Listen, for Logic, for Loyalty, for Magic, for Making love, for Mathematics, for Mechanics, to Mediate, to Merge, to Motivate, to Monitor, to Negotiate, to Nurture, to Obey, to Observe, to Officiate, to Orchestrate, to Order, to Organise, for Originality, to Oversee, to Parenting, to Perceive Intuitively, to Perform, to Persist, to Persuade, for Physical care, to Plan, to Play, for Poetry, to Portray images, for Pragmatism, for Precision, to Preserve, to Protect, for Psychic abilities, to Relate, to Repair, to Represent, to Sanity, to Seduce, to Sell, to Sense, for Serenity, to Smell, to Socialize, for Soil, to Stabilize, to Stage shows, to Study, to Supervise, to Support, to Synthesize, to Taste, to Teach, to Test, to Train, to Trust, to Upkeep, to Uplift, to Visualize, to Verbalize, to Write, for Zealousness.

Made in the USA
San Bernardino, CA
15 December 2016